Mosquitoes

Ouch! – you have been bitten by a flying insect. But what was it? Was it a mosquito, a gnat, or a midge? What makes a mosquito special, and does it really 'bite'? Here you can find out all about these interesting insects, which have caused more deaths than all Man's wars. Some mosquitoes carry diseases like malaria, but others are just irritating as they stab us to suck our blood.

Anthony Wootton tells us about the different kinds of mosquitoes and how they live. This book is illustrated with many black and white photographs and drawings. There is a glossary of words which may be new to you, a section to help you find out more about mosquitoes, and an index.

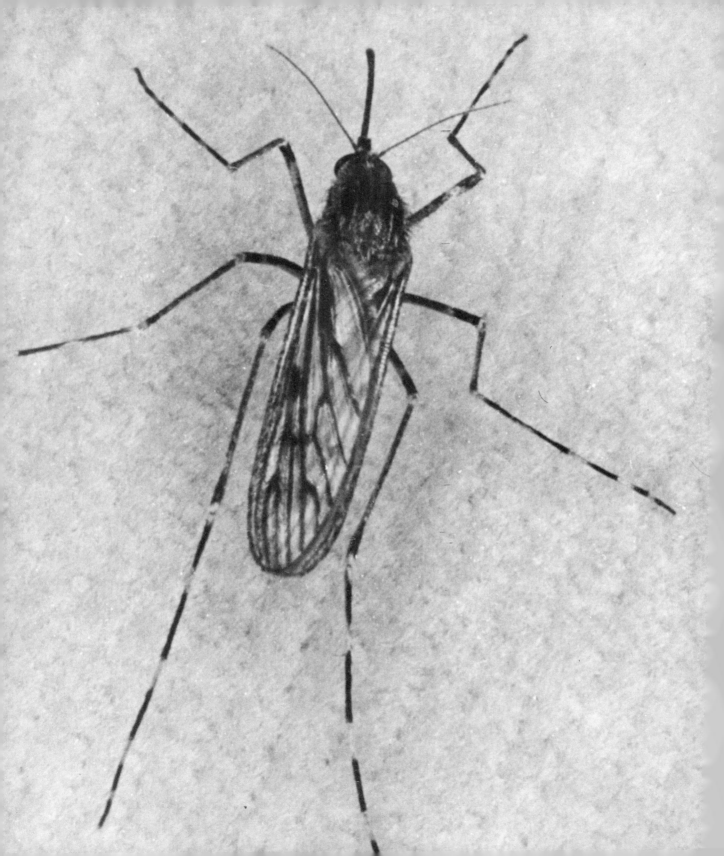

Mosquitoes

Anthony Wootton

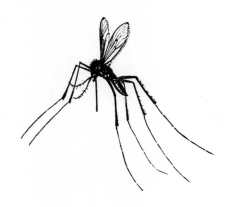

Young Naturalist Books

Foxes
Squirrels
Bats
Snakes and Lizards
Frogs and Toads
Hedgehogs
Badgers
Deer
Rabbits and Hares
Spiders
Otters
Rats and Mice
Stoats and Weasels

Bees and Wasps
Birds of Prey
Ants
Beetles
Pond Life
Crickets and Grasshoppers
Flies
Freshwater Fish
Worms
Mosquitoes
Wild Cats
Ducks
Eels

Frontispiece: **The female *Theobaldia annulata* mosquito hibernates in houses and has a severe, sometimes poisonous, bite.**

First published in 1979 by
Wayland Publishers Limited
49 Lansdowne Place, Hove
East Sussex, BN3 1HF, England

© copyright 1979 Wayland Publishers Limited

ISBN 0 85340 664 2

Typeset by Computacomp (UK) Ltd.
Fort William, Scotland, printed and bound
by The Pitman Press, Bath.

Contents

1 : Mosquitoes, gnats and midges

One of the drawbacks of sitting near a pond, lake or marsh is the likelihood of being bitten by insects like mosquitoes, gnats and midges. You know they are about because they commonly fly with a high-pitched whining sound. You may not know you have been bitten – or rather stabbed – until the attackers have actually taken some of your blood.

These insects keep coming back, however much we swat or wave our arms at them. We squash them as they are in the very act of biting us, but that does not seem to scare the rest away. Their bloodthirsty attacks make us come up in little bumps which itch for hours afterward. In fact human reaction to mosquito bites varies from one person to another – some seem to suffer less than others. By extreme contrast, in many parts of the world mosquitoes may carry deadly diseases, such as malaria.

It is hard to see any good in insects like these – insects which are not content with simply biting us but take a feed of our blood at the

A female Culicine mosquito feeding on human blood.

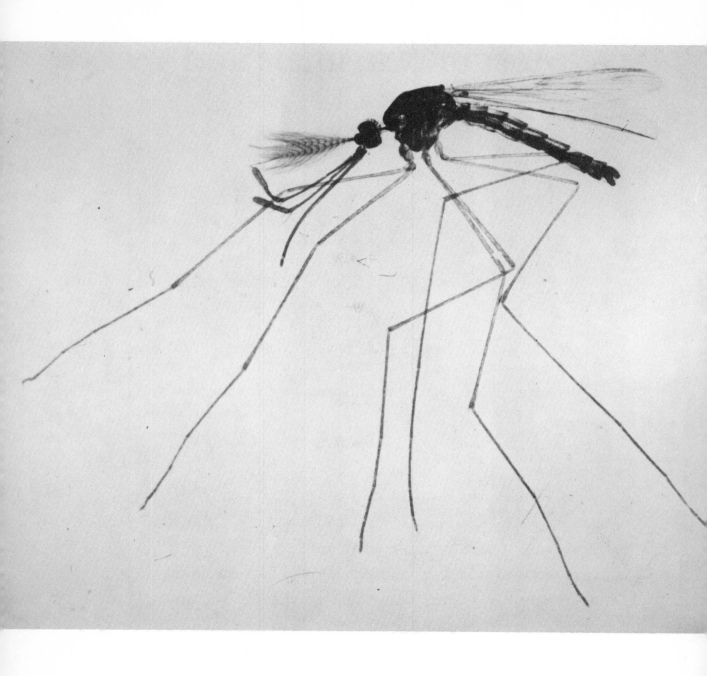

8   Male and female of the mosquito *Anopheles maculipennis*. This is one of the carriers of malaria. Note the feathered antennae. The male is above, the female on the right.

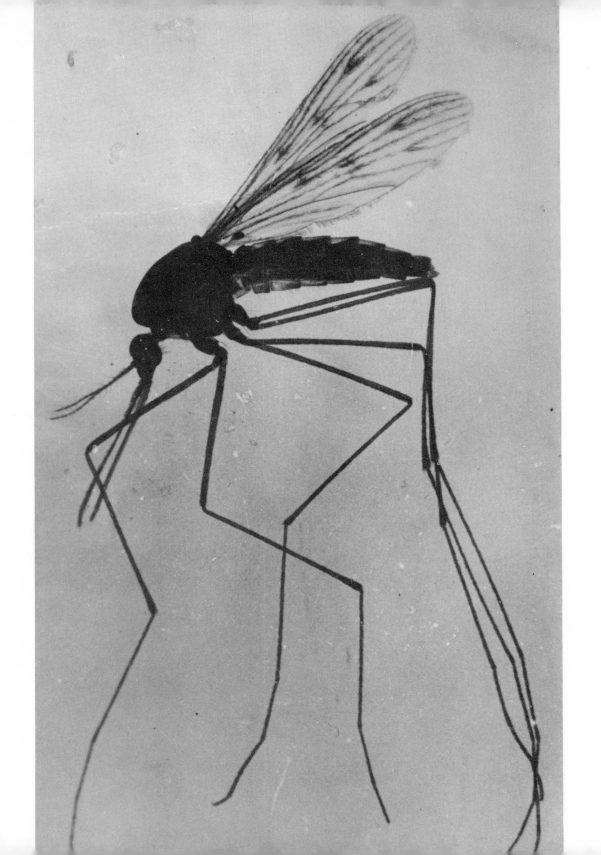

same time. But of course by 'good' we mean good to *us*. We look at the matter only from our point of view. The mosquito is equally selfish. It sees and uses us simply as a means to an end — as you will see in Chapter 3. One thing is certain: a mosquito does not bite us out of ill-will or because we are trespassing on its territory (insects *do* have territories). A meal of blood is essential to the mosquito for a very special reason.

What *are* mosquitoes, and what are the differences between them and gnats and midges? People commonly use these names as if they referred to the same insects. For example, what is widely known as the Common Gnat is really a mosquito (*Culex pipiens*), although it is usually harmless to Man. This is the species you can often see in and around your garden water butt. The word 'gnat' is an Old English word for mosquito. 'Mosquito' is a Spanish word, meaning 'little fly', and seems to have been first used by the Spaniards when they were greatly pestered by these insects during their conquests of Central and South America during the sixteenth century. The name 'midge' is usually reserved for very small flies (not mosquitoes), some of which bite Man, although others are harmless. Common names can be very misleading, and this is why biologists prefer to use their own, scientific ones.

All of these insects have at least one thing in common: they are two-winged flies (*Diptera*). Mosquitoes, however, belong to a fly family all on their own, called the *Culicidae*. Like all Diptera they have only one pair of wings, the hind pair being reduced to little

---

A Chironomid midge or gnat. It is not related to the mosquitoes.

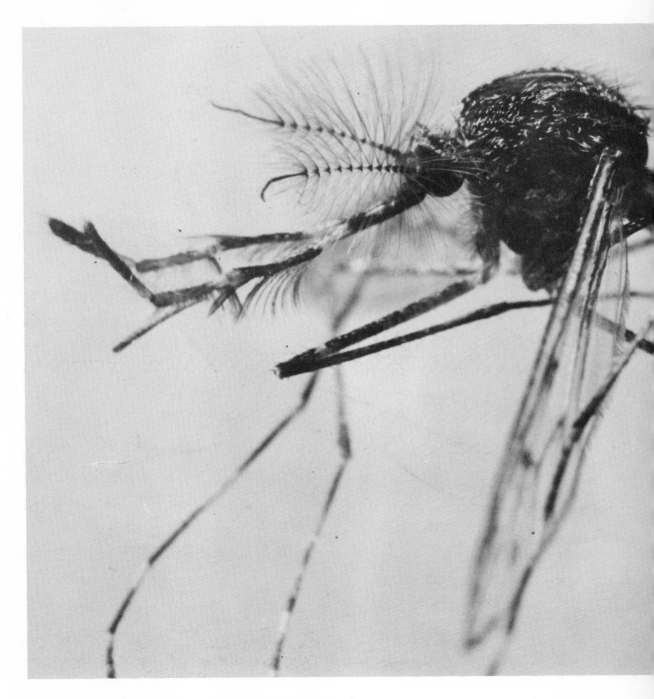

The head of a female mosquito, *Culex pipiens* (left) and male (above).

club-ended processes which may be used as balancers. They vibrate in time with the wings when the insect is flying. Mosquitoes, unlike other flies, have tiny scale-like hairs on the lower edge of their narrow wings and also on the veins. They have long, thin bodies, delicate trailing legs, and long antennae or feelers. In the male these are plumed like little feathers, but in the female they are armed with short peg-like projections. The female has a long proboscis, which she uses to pierce flesh and suck blood. Males have shorter and less specially developed proboscises because they never suck blood but instead feed on plant juices, such as nectar and decaying fruit.

There are about 2,000 species of mosquito in different parts of the world, varying in length from a few millimetres to over four centimetres (about two inches). Most of them occur in warm countries, especially in the tropics, but some can also exist in the polar regions. Britain has about thirty species.

There are two main types of mosquito, one group being called the Culicines, the other the Anophelines. Typical and most familiar of the Culicine group is the Common Gnat, *Culex pipiens*, mentioned earlier, which often undergoes its life cycle in water butts and rainwater tanks. The second part of its scientific name is Latin for 'piping'. It makes a thin high-pitched sound in flight. It rarely bites Man, but concentrates on birds. Some other species in the group, for example, *Culex molestus* are not so particular. One of the worst biters of the group is the large *Theobaldia annulata*, which you can recognize by its long black and white banded legs and body. The females of this species hibernate during the winter, sometimes even in houses. They unfortunately wake up from time to time and take a

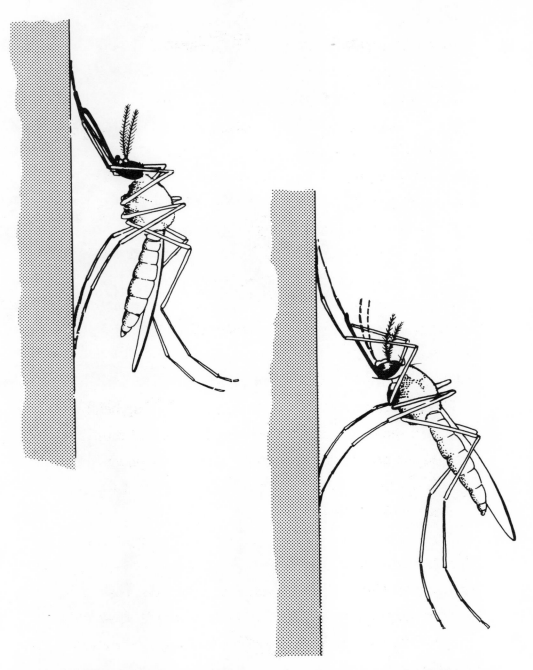

This diagram shows the mosquito's attitude when at rest on the surface. On the right, the Culicine mosquito; on the left, the Anopheline.

Marshlands and ponds
provide a perfect
breeding habitat for
mosquitoes.

feed of blood to keep them going – sometimes from a person asleep in bed! In some foreign countries, certain other Culicines are even more troublesome. *Aedes aegypti*, for example, is the carrier of the terrible disease known as yellow fever.

Anopheline mosquitoes are even more famous. Perhaps 'infamous' or 'notorious' would be a better word, because several of the group cause malaria, probably the world's most dreaded disease. At one time, malaria could be caught in Britain. It is still a great scourge in many other countries, even in parts of Europe.

One can tell the difference between the two types of mosquito from the way they rest on the surface of the water or waterside plants. Culicines like the Common Gnat usually hold their bodies more or less parallel with their resting surface. Anophelines, on the other hand, tilt their bodies forward at an angle, so that they appear to be trying to stand on their head.

Another difference is that Culicine mosquitoes have mostly unpatterned wings, whereas Anophelines have dark spots or blotches on them. It is very hard to identify mosquitoes. It all depends on the arrangement of the veins in their wings, and also on an examination of their internal organs. You will need to study flies seriously to be able to recognize even all of the thirty British species – and this may mean that you will have to get used to being bitten!

2: A watery beginning

You are most likely to be bitten by mosquitoes while near water, as you will have learned in the opening chapter. A mosquito spends its early life as a larva in water, and the female mosquito needs water in which to lay her eggs. Like all insects, mosquitoes pass through a complicated life history, called metamorphosis. This involves great changes in their form – from egg to larva, larva to pupa, and from pupa to adult.

All sorts of water are used by mosquitoes for egg-laying. Depending on the species, it could be ponds or lakes, estuaries or salt marshes, semi-liquid manure, or even puddles in a cart track. Some pass their whole life-cycle in the rainwater which collects in tree boles, or even in the large leaves of some kinds of tropical plants.

The Common Gnat (*Culex pipiens*) often uses garden water butts or rainwater tanks in which to lay her eggs. If you look carefully in summer you may see them: little mats of perhaps 200–300 eggs, each about a millimetre across, joined together and floating like tiny rafts. They are waterproof and unsinkable and will bob back to the

20

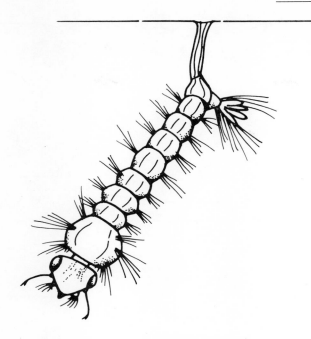

The larva of the Culicine mosquito, (above and left) hanging at the surface of the water. Note the siphon at the end of its body which draws in air.

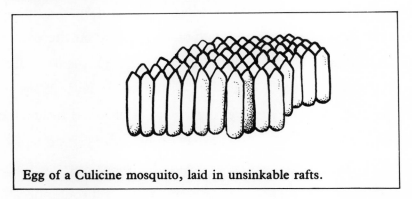

Egg of a Culicine mosquito, laid in unsinkable rafts.

surface however many times you push them under. Anopheline mosquitoes lay their floating eggs singly, so these are much less easy to find. In any case, they are more likely to be laid in larger stretches of water, such as ponds and lakes, which have plenty of water plants in them. There is also a distinct difference between the larvae of the

21

The larva of an Anopheline mosquito.

Egg of an Anopheline mosquito, laid singly.

two groups. The Culicine larva is easy to recognize, despite its small size (about 5 mm.). It has a large head, with compound eyes, and a body made of segments armed with short bristles. At the end of its body is a tube which is joined to it at an angle. This is its breathing tube. It breaks the surface tension of the water and absorbs air, while the larva is, as it were, doing a sort of crooked headstand in the water. Anopheline mosquito larvae do not have this air siphon at one end. They simply lie just beneath the water surface, held in position by their body hairs, and take in air direct through breathing pores at the end of their abdomen, where it breaks through the water surface.

Mosquito larvae do not stay at the surface all the time. They have to move at intervals, both to feed and to escape predators. They swim in a wriggling motion by flexing their abdomen. If you look into a water butt you may see some gnat larvae hanging from the surface, taking in air. The slightest movement, even your shadow, will make them wriggle down into the darker depths out of sight. They soon return, however. They have to or they would drown; the larvae cannot use the air dissolved in the water for breathing.

Mosquito larvae feed on a variety of things. Some eat tiny green plants, such as algae, or minute animals living in the water. Others eat particles of dead matter in the water. They have fringes of hairs or bristles around their mouths which move in a rhythmic motion to draw in food. Some feed at the bottom of the water, others nearer the surface.

The larva feeds for about three weeks; during this time it changes its skin to allow for growth. This is the only way an insect can get bigger. The larva then becomes inactive and changes into the pupa, which is the final stage before it changes into an adult mosquito. The pupa is just as distinctive as the larva. The pupae of all mosquitoes look roughly the same. Hanging at the surface of the water, the pupa is like a little comma (,) in shape, the tail hanging downwards in a curve. The pupa does not feed, but it needs even more oxygen than the larva, so that it rarely leaves the water surface. On the back of its thorax are a pair of little air siphons. These break the surface tension of the water and take in air. The air it breathes out is trapped between the casing of the legs and wings, and this helps it float. If a pupa is taken out of the water and this air bubble is removed, the pupa will sink. The mosquito pupa is almost as active as the larva, and can wriggle rapidly through the water by bending its abdomen forwards and back.

23

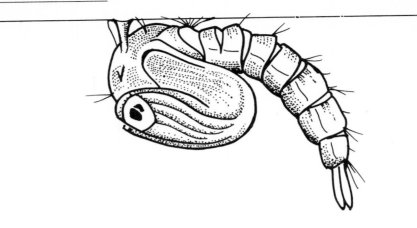

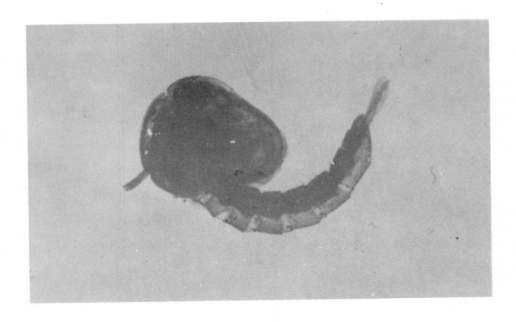

The pupa of an Anopheline mosquito. The little 'trumpets' at the top are air siphons.

A mosquito spends about three or four days as a pupa – a much shorter time than it spends as a larva. When the time comes for the adult winged insect to emerge, the pupa stretches itself horizontally beneath the water surface, splits open at the thorax, and the adult struggles out. It may rest on the pupal case while expanding and drying its wings and body, although it can stand on the water using its surface tension. Adult mosquitoes are in great danger from predators, such as birds, at this critical time of their life. This is partly because if they flew away too soon their wings would not beat fast enough to make the right sound for them to be recognized by other mosquitoes of the same species. It is vital that mosquitoes do recognize each other, for otherwise mating might not take place. Each mosquito species beats its wings at a particular speed. In females this is usually from about 450 to 600 beats per second. A male can recognize the particular sound by means of his specially feathered antennae, which act like a radio aerial. His antennae vibrate in response to the sound. He can recognize what kind of sound it is and where it comes from. There is a special organ for this purpose at the base of each antenna. If the sound is of the wrong frequency, the male simply ignores it, but if it is right he zooms in on his partner and mates with her. It is now that the female is ready for her first feed of blood.

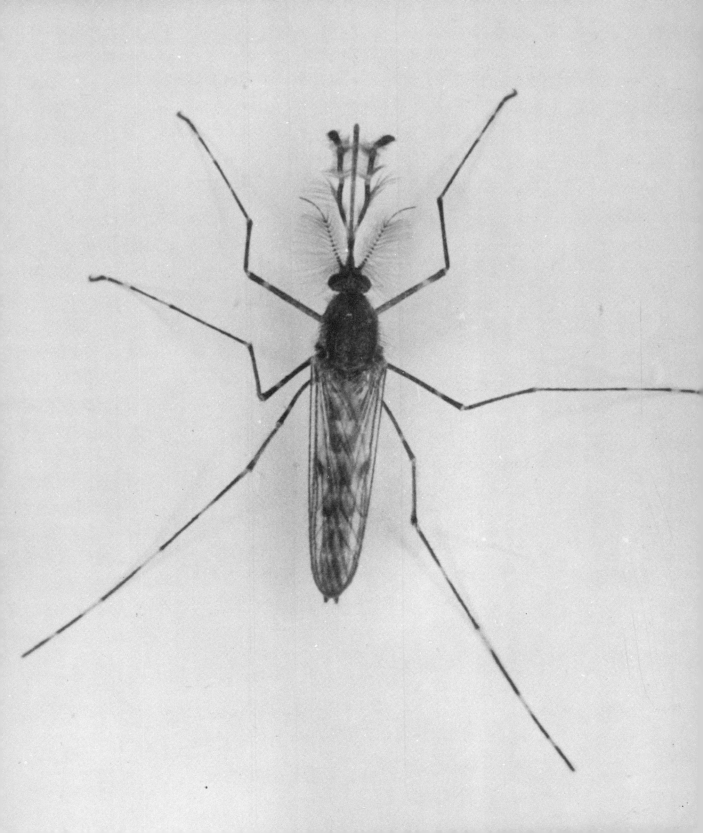

3 : Insect bloodsuckers

You may not appreciate the fact at the time, perhaps, but the way a mosquito withdraws our blood is really wonderfully delicate and clever. It is far more precise and skilful than the work of any human surgeon. No scalpel or hypodermic syringe could be compared to the mosquito's proboscis. What looks like a single, thin stabbing tube is really made of *six* different parts called 'stylets'. All of them are contained in a special sheath. It is almost as if the mosquito carried its own box of surgical instruments about with it.

When the mosquito has found a suitable victim, it first explores its body surface with the sensitive tip of its proboscis. Then the proboscis is inserted. As this happens, the sheath slides up out of the way, bending in a loop as you can see in the diagram. Now the various working parts of the proboscis begin the task of extracting the blood. The initial incision of the skin is made by two pairs of needle-sharp stylets. One of these pairs has saw-like tips which

Male *Theobaldia annulata*. Unlike the female, males die when the colder weather comes. Note the feathered antennae.

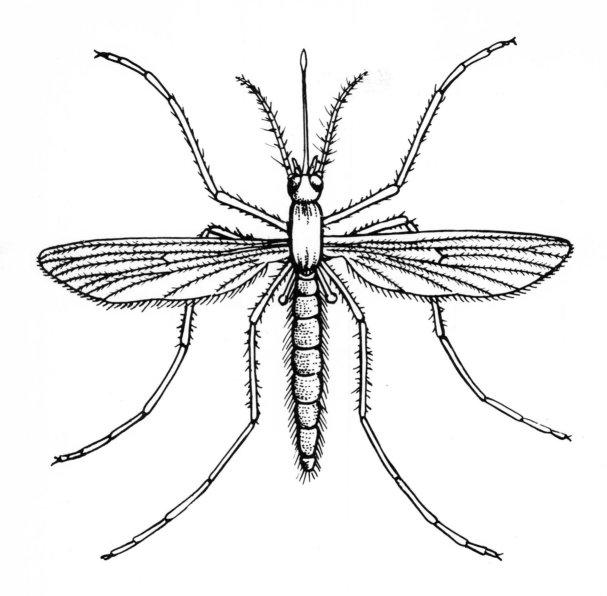

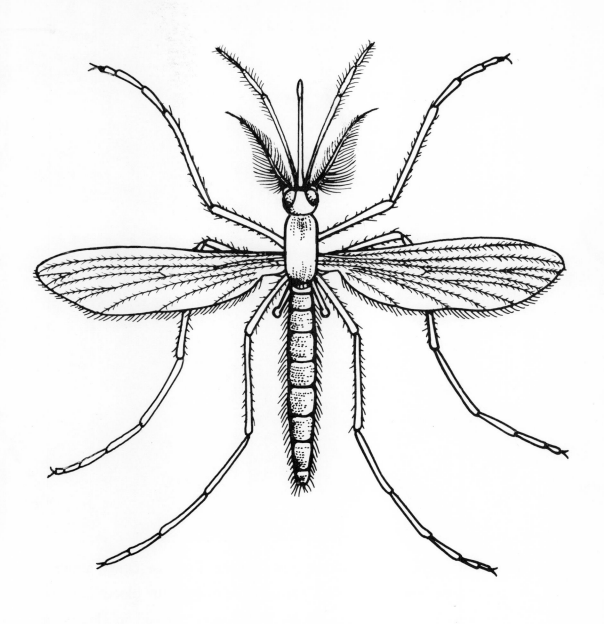

Female and male mosquito, generalized to show the different antennae. The female is on the left, male on the right.

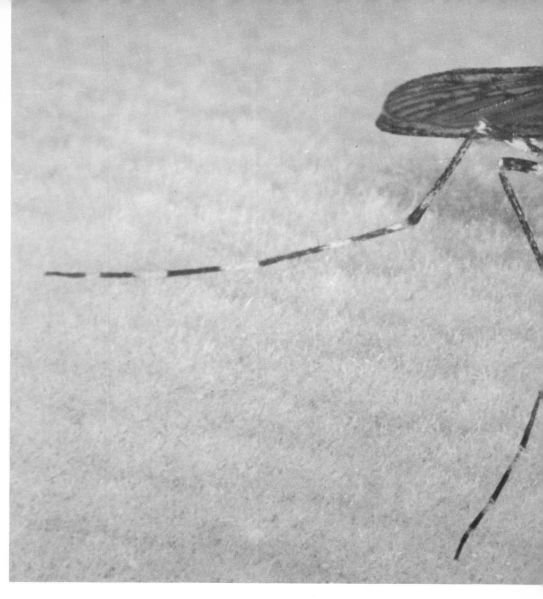

anchor in the flesh; another pair has piercing tips. Down another stylet tube flows saliva. This partially pre-digests the blood and also prevents it from clotting. If the blood were allowed to clot, as it normally does when you cut or graze yourself, the mosquito would be unable to obtain its meal. It is probably the saliva, too, which causes the itching we feel after a mosquito bite.

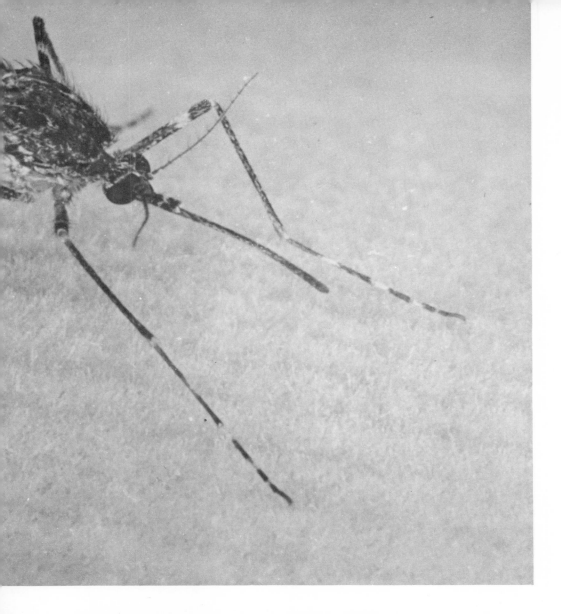

Female *Theobaldia annulata*. This large species often hibernates in houses and has a severe, but rarely dangerous, bite.

After the skin has been punctured and the saliva injected, the sixth and last stylet gets to work. This is the 'upper lip' which draws the blood into the mosquito's body. The whole operation is

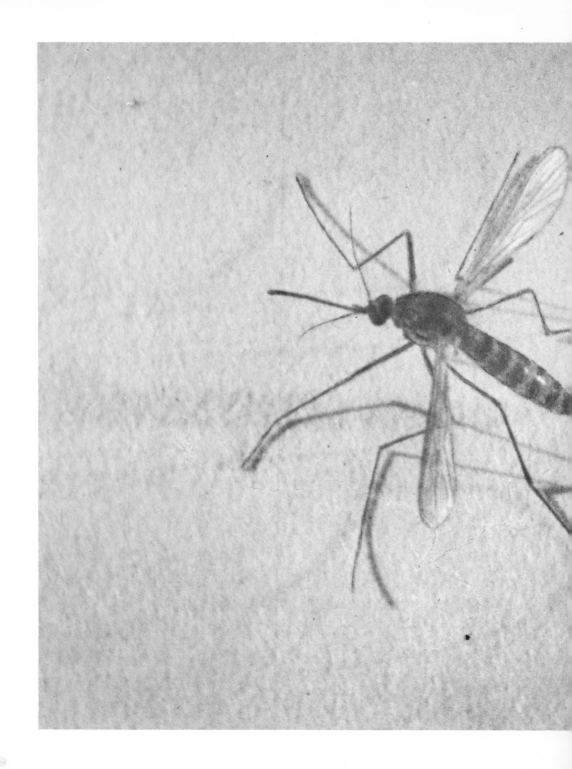

The Common Gnat, *Culex pipiens*. This species rarely bites people but prefers to attack birds.

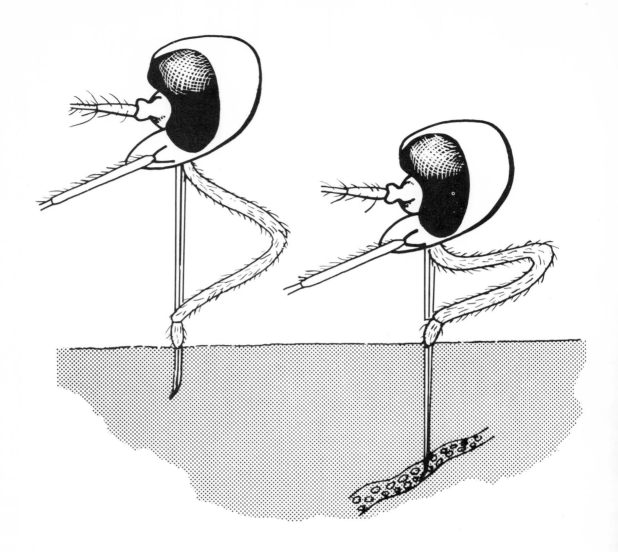

This is how the mouthparts move when the female stabs for blood.

completed in a very short space of time, during which the mosquito may absorb its own body weight in blood.

A mosquito doesn't take our blood simply as food. It needs blood to be able to lay its eggs. Biologists think that blood helps the mosquito produce eggs by giving it essential foods, such as proteins.

It is possible for some mosquitoes to lay eggs *without* taking blood, but usually far *more* eggs are laid if the mosquito has fed in this way. In some species blood is essential.

If it is any comfort to you, we are not the only creatures to be attacked by mosquitoes. Wild and domestic mammals are stabbed, and so are birds, reptiles and amphibians, insects, and animals like crabs. Most of these animals have very little defence against the mosquito's attack. We can at least swat them, use repellent sprays and creams, or sleep under mosquito netting.

A mosquito's attack is extremely subtle. Many make a high-pitched whine, caused by the vibration of their wings, which warn us they are near. Others are quieter because their wing-beats are faster and the sound they produce is beyond our hearing range. In any case, no such noise is produced when the insect has found a suitable host. It settles on us unnoticed, with the lightness of the lightest feather. Sometimes we are not even aware of having been bitten until some time afterwards. This is because the mosquito's saliva contains a sort of anesthetic which prevents our feeling any itching until the mosquito has left. The mosquito also seems to choose a place to stab where we are not very sensitive.

There are several ways mosquitoes can detect their 'prey'. If they are day-active species, they can see their victims with their large compound eyes. These are really only good for noticing movement and shape: they cannot focus. More important, a mosquito can detect the smell of our bodies, and also tell we are near by the higher temperature and the carbon dioxide we give off. It has special chemo-receptors all along the length of its antennae to do this job. A

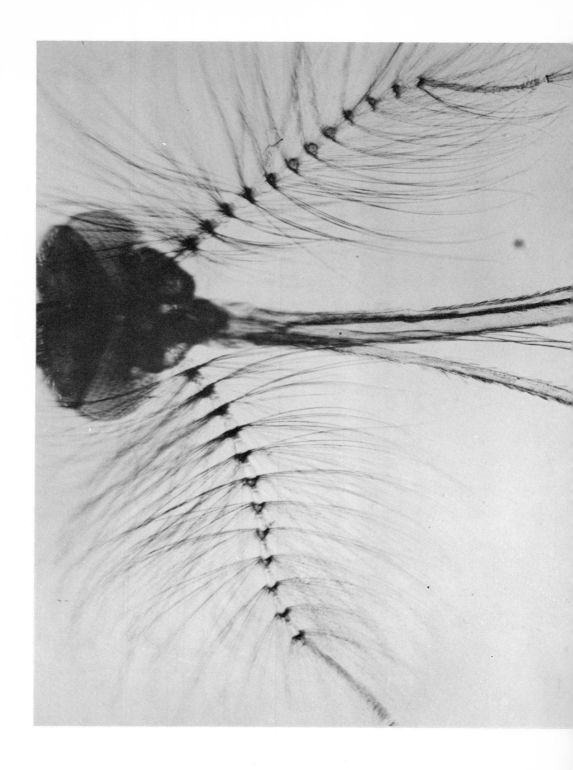

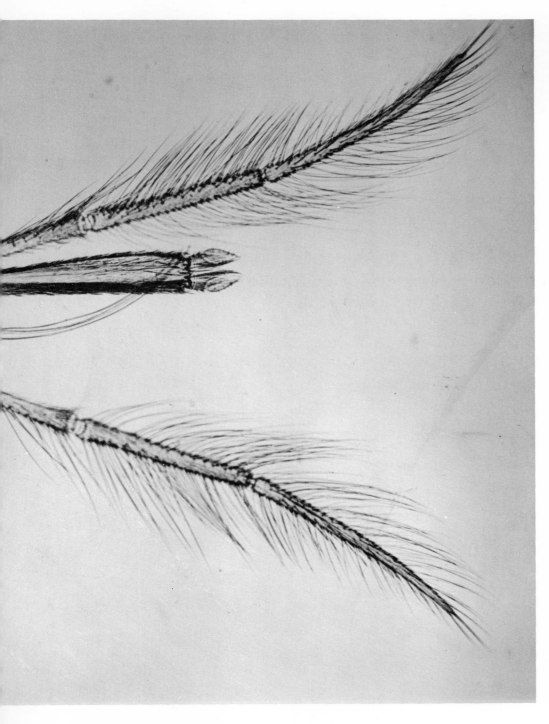

The mouthparts of this male *Culex pipiens* are not adapted for blood-sucking—only for sipping plant juices.

37

mosquito is very sensitive to humidity — that is, a combination of warmth and moisture. This is why people who perspire a lot are far more likely to be bitten than those who do not. I have found this out for myself. I was exploring the lake region of southern Czechoslovakia some years ago with two companions. I was bitten so badly by mosquitoes that my bare arms became covered with blood; but my companions, who seemed able to stay cool, were almost untouched.

Your chances of being bitten also vary according to the part of the world in which you live. In northern countries and temperate climates, where the winter season is marked, mosquitoes only bite in warmer weather. In the tropics, where it is warm all year round, mosquitoes are active all the time. New generations of biting mosquitoes are continually emerging, and human beings and animals are given little peace from their attacks. During all this blood-letting activity, the males take no blood at all but just nectar and fruit juices of various kinds. This goes to show the truth of the old saying about the female of the species being deadlier than the male. The truly deadly nature of the (female) mosquito will be shown even more clearly in Chapter 5, which tells of the diseases caused by its bites.

4 : Few survive

Only a few of the hundreds of eggs laid by the adult females ever become adults. Fortunately for us, they have many enemies, otherwise we should be absolutely plagued with them! This is why insects lay so many eggs; if they produced only a few, and they were eaten, the species would soon die out. As it is, there is a sort of safety – or survival value – in numbers.

Actually, mosquito *eggs* may survive quite well, since they are hard and not attractive to eat. As soon as they produce soft-bodied larvae a whole army of enemies is just waiting to snap them up as food. They are eaten by an enormous variety of water animals, such as fish, frogs, newts, carnivorous water beetles, bugs and dragonfly larvae, to name but a few. Dragonfly larvae, or nymphs, have a very spectacular method of capturing them. They shoot out a kind of 'mask' armed with fangs which impale the victim, which is then drawn back into the larva's mouth. Mosquito larvae even fall victim to certain kinds of carnivorous plants. The bladderwort, for example, captures them by means of special bladders arranged along its underwater stems, each of them armed with little hairs

which trigger off a sort of sucking siphon when touched. Once inside the bladders, the plant is able to digest the larvae.

Even if they manage to survive all these hazards as larvae and pupae, mosquitoes are still in danger when they become adults. Many are eaten as soon as they emerge from the pupa. You have probably seen swallows, swifts and martins swooping down to pick

Newts are among the many enemies of mosquitoes.

off insects from the surface of ponds and lakes. Much of these birds'
prey will be mosquitoes just taking their first look at the outside
world.

Mosquitoes are just as threatened when they take to the air. Birds

Adult and larva of great diving beetle. This large beetle is a predator at both adult and larva stage.

43

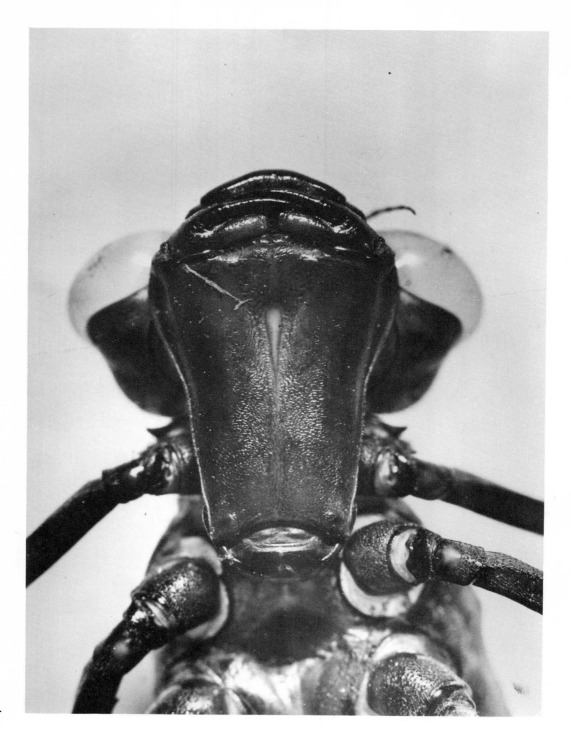

44

Dragonfly larvae or nymphs capture their prey, including mosquito larvae, in a strange way. They shoot out a sort of hinged mask armed with pincers, as shown on the left.

---

like flycatchers seize them in full flight, as do swift-flying dragonflies. At night, bats may capture them, using their own form of radar. They emit pulses which bounce off the mosquito, return to the bat, and tell it just where its prey is, all in the twinkling of an eye. If they venture near the ground, they may get entangled in spiders' webs. There are even certain kinds of spiders which do not

Above: The bladderwort is an animal-eating plant which catches and digests mosquito larvae.

Right: Flycatchers, like this pied flycatcher, are adept at catching mosquitoes in flight.

make webs but simply run down the mosquitoes on the surface of the water. Most remarkable mosquito-predators of all, perhaps, are certain biting midges. They prey on mosquitoes by piercing the abdomen and robbing it of the blood it has extracted. Rather a case of dog eats dog!

Because it carries diseases of various kinds, the mosquito has yet another, even more important enemy to contend with – Man. Mosquitoes are rarely more than annoying in Britain, but in other countries their bite can kill or at least make the victim very sick, and

47

Birds like these sand martins take many newly-emerged mosquitoes from the surface of the water.

Above: The water spider captures adult mosquitoes on the surface of the water.

Left: Another mosquito enemy: the water boatman. It feeds on its prey by injecting a digestive juice and sucking out its victim's tissues.

so all sorts of methods are used to control them. Breeding areas may be sprayed with poisons like D.D.T., or oil may be pumped on to the breeding waters or marshes to prevent the larvae emerging. Marshes are also drained for a similar reason.

In spite of all these dangers to their survival, mosquitoes still survive in large numbers. They remain one of the most troublesome

51

Most freshwater fish, including these trout fry, will eat mosquito larvae and pupae.

of insect pests. As we have seen, they lay enough eggs so that even if they lose vast numbers of their population, they still survive as a species. Their ability to develop in all sorts of waters, even small puddles, is another reason for their success. Mosquitoes have many other methods of surviving difficult conditions. Some species can hibernate. Adult fertilized females go into a sort of coma during the winter months, when their breathing rate is so low that they use up very little energy. Then they awake the following spring to lay their eggs. Others *aestivate*. This is a sort of dry weather hibernation; the insects go into 'suspended animation' when it is too dry for egg-laying and development. Eggs of some desert-living species are very resistant to drought. They may remain unhatched for long periods until the right conditions occur – sometimes this is as long as several years!

Like many insects, mosquitoes are also able to move off and start a new life in other areas, perhaps many kilometres away. This is rarely deliberate, because they are not strong fliers. But they are so light, even when gorged with blood, that they may be blown great distances by winds, after spiralling upwards in warm air currents (thermals). This may often explain why there are sudden outbreaks of disease in places where it was previously rare or unknown.

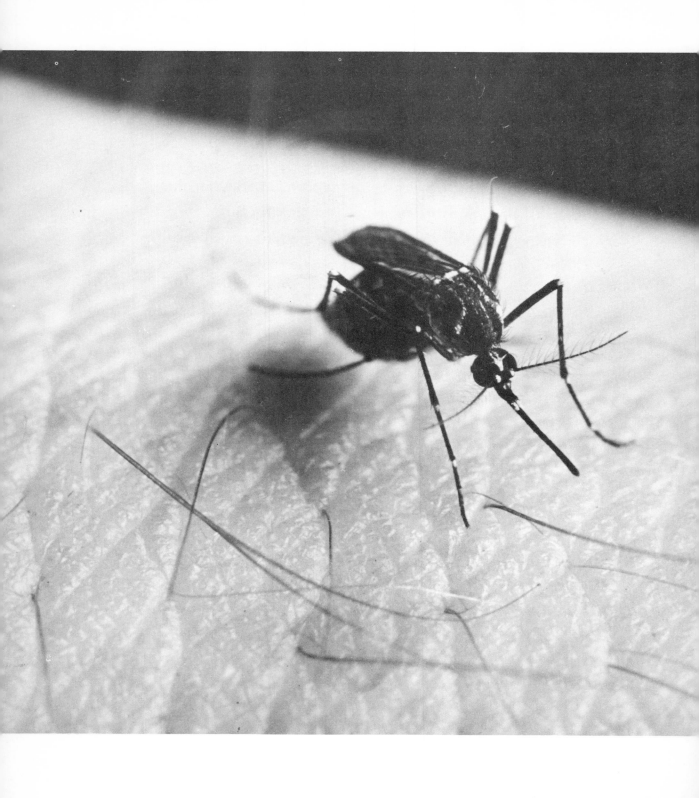

5 : Disease carriers

If I were to say that a little insect like the mosquito has been the cause of more human deaths and suffering than all Man's wars put together, you would probably shake your head in disbelief. Nevertheless, it is a fact. Malaria, carried only by certain kinds of Anopheline mosquitoes, has killed millions of people and made countless others very ill ever since the beginning of history. It has reduced the populations of countries, wiped out cities, decided the outcome of battles, stopped work on great building projects, and interfered with Man's doings in countless other ways. Malaria greatly hampered explorers of many parts of the world. Central Africa, for example, was called 'the white man's grave' because of the risk of catching this and other diseases. Despite improved methods of mosquito control and malaria treatment, malaria is still the greatest single cause of death, especially in countries like India. It has been estimated that there are something like 250 million cases

The mosquito *Aedes aegypti* about to feed from a human arm. This is the species which carries the yellow fever parasite.

In tropical and mediterranean areas, mosquitoes can be controlled by spraying their breeding waters with paraffin.

57

of malaria in the world every year, about 3 million of which prove fatal. Mosquito control costs millions of pounds every year. Even now, mosquitoes prevent us from living in many parts of the world.

The curious thing about all this is that the mosquito itself is virtually innocent! It is merely the *carrier* of the disease, which it picks up and passes on unknowingly. Just as we may have some infectious complaint and pass it on to a friend, perhaps even before we have begun to feel ill, so the mosquito has no idea of causing our sickness when it takes a feed of blood. It bites only to obtain food for itself and the proper development of its eggs.

The trouble is caused by a minute, single-celled animal called *Plasmodium*, which lives in the mosquito's blood and digestive system. Unfortunately for us, the *Plasmodium* cannot complete its life cycle in the mosquito but needs a second host — which is usually Man (although certain other kinds of animal, such as monkeys, can also be infected). When a mosquito bites someone, therefore, and injects some of its saliva, the *Plasmodium* may be transferred into the host's system, causing malaria.

We have not always known this, of course. Centuries ago, people believed that diseases like malaria were caused by the foul-smelling air of places like swamps. Indeed, this is the meaning of the word malaria, which derives from the Italian words *mala* (bad) and *aria* (air). People did not connect malaria with mosquitoes.

The truth about the relationship between mosquitoes and malaria only came to light less than a century ago. It had long been

Spraying the tents of the nomadic Kurds with D.D.T.

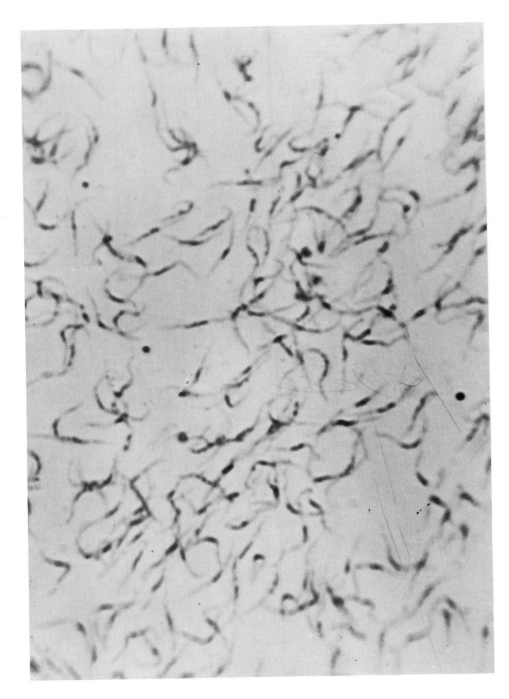

The plasmodium parasite – the real cause of malaria.

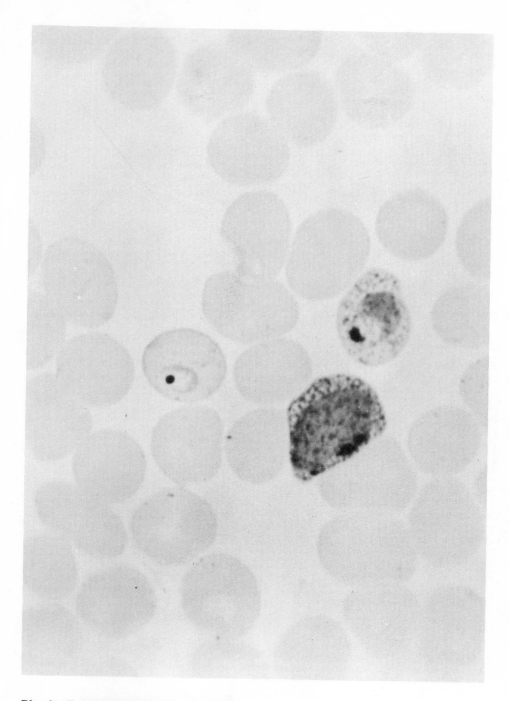

Blood cells infected with the malarial parasite.

established that mosquitoes carried the disease, but what was puzzling was that not *all* seemed to do so. A man might be bitten by a mosquito and yet not get the disease. In order to control it, more specific information was needed. Here two men in particular deserve our gratitude for making the situation clear. One of them was Sir Ronald Ross (1857–1932) who during the 1890s worked as an army doctor for the Indian Medical Service. After much painstaking research, he and his friend Sir Patrick Manson (1844–1922) not only isolated the malarial parasite but also found that it was only carried by certain kinds of Anopheline mosquito. Nor was that the end of the matter. A mosquito might be quite free of the malarial parasite, but if it bit an infected person, withdrawing some of his blood, it became a carrier – able to infect another healthy person when it took some of *his* blood.

The knowledge gained by men like Ross and Manson opened the way for other researchers to combat equally dreadful diseases, such as yellow fever, dengue, filariasis and elephantiasis, all of which are carried by certain kinds of mosquito. Yellow fever, for example, is transmitted by the Culicid mosquito *Aedes aegypti*. This was the disease which caused the original French attempts to build the Panama Canal to be abandoned.

Nowadays we have many ways of combating these diseases. We can isolate malarial sufferers and thus prevent mosquitoes from biting them and passing on the disease. We can use substances like quinine which, together with certain recently discovered synthetic drugs, kills the malarial parasite in the human bloodstream. We can also kill the malarial carriers — that is, the mosquitoes — with chemicals and by various other means. Malaria has been virtually wiped out in Britain because sufferers from the disease rarely find their way into this country, or if they do are quickly isolated. We can even stop the mosquitoes' irritating bites by using creams and aerosol sprays. These tend to confuse the mosquito and make it look for another host.

Unfortunately, problems arise in trying to control mosquitoes in their natural habitat. By spraying with oil or D.D.T. we may also kill useful animals. This has happened several times, with disastrous effects on the local ecology. Mosquitoes, like many insects, tend to develop new hardier strains, resistant to the latest pesticides. It may be that the future of mosquito- and malaria-control lies in more subtle methods. For example, certain kinds of fish, such as the guppy, have been introduced into areas with malaria to eat the mosquito larvae. Experiments have also been made to attract mosquitoes in large numbers by playing sounds of the same frequency as their wing-beats. Another move has been to release laboratory-sterilized male mosquitoes, so that when they mate with the females only infertile eggs will result. Man's fight against the mosquito still goes on. Whether or not he will win in the end is still a matter for doubt.

Sir Patrick Manson

Glossary

ABDOMEN. The hind part of a mosquito's body, containing the digestive and sexual organs.

AESTIVATION. Period of dormancy during summer or dry season.

AGUE. An old name for malarial fever.

ALGAE. Minute aquatic plants found in fresh and salt water.

ANTENNAE. Pair of feelers on the mosquito's head, used for smelling etc. and in the male for receiving the vibrations of a female's wing-beats.

CHEMO-RECEPTOR. Small organs on a mosquito's antennae, which can interpret smell, taste, humidity etc.

COMPOUND EYE. One of a pair of insect eyes, each of which is made up of many linked simple lenses.

D.D.T. DichloroDiphenylTrichloroethane: a pesticide used to control mosquitoes and other insects. It is very persistent and may kill other harmless animals and cause sterility (inability to breed) in others.

DIPTERA. The insect order to which mosquitoes and other two-winged flies belong.

HIBERNATION. Period of inactivity experienced by insects during the winter months.

LARVA. The active feeding stage of an insect like a mosquito.

METAMORPHOSIS. (Literally change of shape). The whole life history of an insect, from egg to adult.

PARASITE. An animal or plant which lives on or in another species.

PREDATOR. An animal which feeds or preys on another.

PROBOSCIS. Collective name for the piercing/sucking mouthparts of an insect like a mosquito.

PROTEIN. Food substance mainly concerned with growing and repairing cells.

PUPA. The final development stage during which an adult mosquito is formed.

QUININE. Substance extracted from the bark of various species of *Cinchona* trees and used to treat malaria.

SALIVA. Digestive fluid used by the mosquito to partly digest blood and prevent it from clotting.

SPECIES. One kind of insect usually able to breed only with another of its kind. For example, *Culex pipiens* and *Anopheles maculipennis* are different species of mosquito which cannot interbreed.

SPIRACLES. Tiny openings on an insect's body through which a passage of air occurs.

SURFACE TENSION. A property of liquid surfaces which makes them behave as if they were coated by a thin film.

THORAX. The middle section of an insect's body which in the adult bears the wings and legs.

Finding out more

After reading about all the distress mosquitoes can cause, you may not feel like making a field study of those species of mosquito which are liable to bite you! There is very little danger of your catching any disease from them, but in any case there is one common species whose life cycle can be easily studied without your having to go any further than the end of the garden *or* risk being bitten. This is *Culex pipiens*, the Common Gnat. It has a worldwide distribution and likes nothing better than to lay its eggs in rainwater tanks or water butts. It is also harmless to Man.

Culex pipiens can of course be studied out of doors. In summer, with luck and patience, you may actually see the females laying their eggs in the water, or observe the adult insects emerging from the pupae. Detailed studies, however, are best made indoors, in a small aquarium or fish tank. This will need to be fairly thin to allow close observation – the eggs, larvae and pupae are very small. The tank can be filled almost to the top. It is best covered with fine gauze or perforated zinc to prevent the adults emerging and escaping before you have had a chance to record when it happened.

If you use the same water you found the mosquitoes in, there will be enough minute items of food in it to keep the larvae going for some days, although it will need to be changed at intervals. You might collect some water or water plants from a pond or lake. In this way, a richer variety of food may be introduced. You may even find some other kinds of mosquito larvae!

There are a number of points worth observing and recording about your captive mosquitoes. For instance, record how long the life cycle takes, from the hatching of the eggs to the emergence of the adult, how long a larva stays at the surface, how long it stays away from it (to feed), and so on. A good idea would be to use a large magnifying glass on a flexible stand. This can easily be positioned and focused so that the developing mosquitoes can be studied more conveniently without too much strain on the eyes.

You may find it helpful to read these books:

A Mosquito is Born by William White Jr. (Sterling/Oak Tree Press).

The British Mosquitoes by J. F. Marshall (Natural History Museum).

British Blood-sucking Flies by F. W. Edwards, H. Oldroyd and J. Smart (Natural History Museum).

Insects and Hygiene by J. R. Busvine (Methuen).

A Handbook for the Identification of Insects of Medical Importance by J. Smart (Natural History Museum).

Mankind Against the Killers by James Hemming (Longmans).

Flies of the British Isles by C. N. Colyer and C. O. Hammond (Warne).

The Natural History of Flies by H. Oldroyd (Weidenfeld & Nicolson).

Insects of the World by W. Linsenmaier (McGraw-Hill).

Index

Picture
Acknowledgements

Heather Angel, 16–17, 20, 40, 41, 42, 43, 44, 52; George Hyde, 12, 13; Natural History Photographic Agency, frontispiece, 6, 11, 26, 30–31, 32–3, 36–7, 50, 55; John Topham, 8, 9, 24, 45, 47; United Nations/World Health Organization, 56, 57, 58; The Wellcome Institute, 60, 61, 62, 65.
Line drawings by Alan Gunston.
The publishers wish to thank the author for the loan of the picture on page 51, and for obtaining that on page 46 which was taken by John Clegg.